The DECLARATION of INDEPENDENCE

250TH ANNIVERSARY GUIDE

Campana

The unanimous Declaration of the thirteen united States of America is a historical document in the public domain in the USA and around the world.

New content for this publication was written, edited and produced by the Campana Press publications team.

publishing@campanapress.com

ISBN: 978-1-0681947-0-2

Typeset in Hoefler Text, Garamond and Goudy Old Style.

Suggested Citation (APA style):

Campana Press Publications. (2025). *The Declaration of Independence: 250th anniversary guide*. Campana Press.

About the Text of the Declaration

The 250-year history of the United States of America can be traced to a one-page document comprising fewer than 1400 words, written in 1776.

The text of the Declaration of Independence in this book is a faithful reproduction, in modern typography, of the engrossed manuscript—the handwritten parchment prepared by Timothy Matlack between July 4 and August 2, 1776, formally adopted with the signatures of the 56 signers. This is the original manuscript of the Declaration, on display today in the National Archives Building in Washington, D.C.

This book reproduces the manuscript precisely, including original spelling, capitalization and punctuation such as colons and long dashes. The source is the 1823 Stone engraving of the signed parchment—see Figure 1.

The Cover Painting

Declaration of Independence (1818) by John Trumbull depicts the Committee of Five presenting the first draft of the Declaration of Independence to the president of the Second Continental Congress, John Hancock, in the Pennsylvania State House, Friday June 28, 1776.

Left to right: John Adams (MA), Roger Sherman (CT), Robert R. Livingston (NY), Thomas Jefferson (VA), Benjamin Franklin (PA). This enormous painting, measuring 18 x 12 feet, has been on permanent display in the U.S. Capitol rotunda, Washington, D.C., since 1826.

Numbered Illustrations

Contents

"These are the times that try men's souls.
The summer soldier and the sunshine patriot will,
in this crisis, shrink from the service of their
country; but he that stands by it now, deserves the
love and thanks of man and woman."

Thomas Paine
The American Crisis
December 23, 1776

The Declaration of Independence

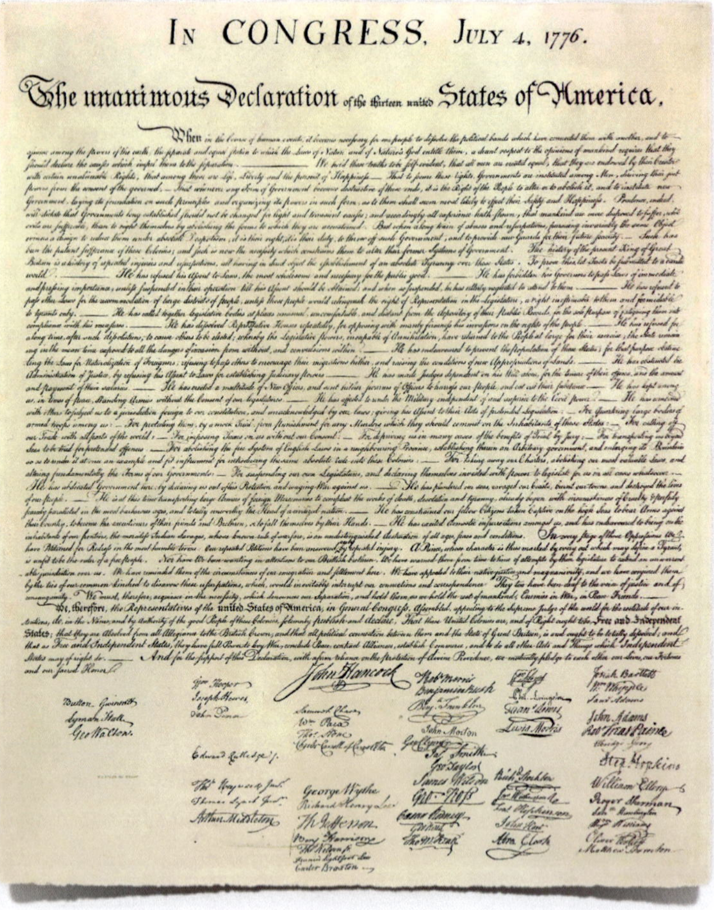

IN CONGRESS, JULY 4, 1776.

The unanimous Declaration of the thirteen united States of America,

Figure 1: The Declaration of Independence

The 1823 Stone engraving is a perfect facsimile of the signed manuscript of the Declaration—an exact copy of the original parchment, as signed by the 56 Congressional delegates. It is named for its printer, William J. Stone.

In CONGRESS, July 4, 1776.

The unanimous Declaration of the thirteen united States of America,

When in the Course of human events, it becomes necessary for one people to dissolve the political bands which have connected them with another, and to assume among the powers of the earth, the separate and equal station to which the Laws of Nature and of Nature's[1] God entitle them, a decent respect to the opinions of mankind requires that they should declare the causes which impel them to the separation. —

[1] "Laws of Nature and of Nature's God": This phrase introduces the idea that the Declaration is grounded in the highest of moral laws, portraying these as superior to any man-made authority—including the British King. They are a fundamental justification for the Declaration based on Enlightenment thinking about natural law. Note, too, the claim that the people of these "thirteen united States" are "equal in station" (position) to all other peoples on earth.

We hold these truths to be self-evident, that all men are created equal,[2] that they are endowed by their Creator with certain unalienable Rights, that among these are Life, Liberty and the pursuit of Happiness.[3] ____

That to secure these rights, Governments are instituted among Men, deriving their just powers from the consent of the governed,[4] ____

That whenever any Form of Government becomes destructive of these ends, it is the Right of the People to alter or to abolish it, and to institute new Government, laying its foundation on such

---

[2] "all men are created equal": This foundational claim of the Declaration echoes the *Second Treatise of Government* by the English philosopher John Locke (1632–1704). He imagines a State of Nature where all humans are born equally free, since no one in this state can claim any natural authority over any other. This 18th-century view of equality contrasts with some modern ideas that may include social or economic equality.

[3] The most quoted passage in the Declaration is probably the most famous political statement in history. The original phrase "sacred and undeniable" became "self-evident", apparently suggested by Benjamin Franklin. This simpler wording implies that no further discussion is needed regarding the rights all humans are born with.

[4] On November 19, 1863, Abraham Lincoln paraphrased this line from the Declaration in the Gettysburg Address: "…that government of the people, by the people, for the people, shall not perish from the earth."

principles and organizing its powers in such form, as to them shall seem most likely to effect their Safety and Happiness.

Prudence, indeed, will dictate that Governments long established should not be changed for light and transient causes; and accordingly all experience hath shewn, that mankind are more disposed to suffer, while evils are sufferable, than to right themselves by abolishing the forms to which they are accustomed.[5]

But when a long train of abuses and usurpations, pursuing invariably the same Object evinces a design to reduce them under absolute Despotism, it is their right, it is their duty, to throw off such Government, and to provide new Guards for their future security. ——

Such has been the patient sufferance of these Colonies; and such is now the necessity which

[5] Here the Declaration clarifies that the 13 colonies do not make this momentous decision lightly. By acknowledging people's tendency to endure temporary suffering rather than overturn familiar systems of government, the text presents their case as exceptional—justifying the break from British rule as both considered and necessary.

constrains[6] them to alter their former Systems of Government.

The history of the present King of Great Britain is a history of repeated injuries and usurpations, all having in direct object the establishment of an absolute Tyranny over these States.

To prove this, let Facts be submitted to a candid world.[7] ____

He has refused his Assent to Laws, the most wholesome and necessary for the public good.[8] ____

---

[6] "constrains": This word is carefully chosen to suggest that the colonies' decision has been forced and compelled—they are left with no other choice after all their "patient sufferances".

[7] The Declaration aims to respectfully persuade all potential readers: not just the British, but other States and powers with whom the newly united States will want to have good relations. Hence, Facts are "submitted to a candid world": a world expected to be open and honest in its judgment. The first sentence of the Declaration makes the same polite appeal, with its "decent respect to the opinions of mankind".

[8] The list of 27 grievances against the King begins. These are not mere complaints, but justifications for the historic decision being made. The first grievance accuses George III of refusing Assent to good Laws: in the British system, the tradition was—and still is—that the Monarch gives formal approval to laws enacted by the legislature (Parliament).

He has forbidden his Governors to pass Laws of immediate and pressing importance, unless suspended in their operation till his Assent should be obtained; and when so suspended, he has utterly neglected to attend to them. ——

He has refused to pass other Laws for the accommodation of large districts of people, unless those people would relinquish the right of Representation in the Legislature, a right inestimable to them and formidable to tyrants only. ——

He has called together legislative bodies at places unusual, uncomfortable, and distant from the depository of their public Records, for the sole purpose of fatiguing them into compliance with his measures. ——

He has dissolved Representative Houses repeatedly, for opposing with manly firmness his invasions on the rights of the people. ——

He has refused for a long time, after such dissolutions, to cause others to be elected; whereby the Legislative powers, incapable of Annihilation, have returned to the People at large for their exercise; the State remaining in the mean time exposed to all the dangers of invasion from without, and convulsions within.[9] ___

He has endeavoured to prevent the population of these States; for that purpose obstructing the Laws for Naturalization of Foreigners; refusing to pass others to encourage their migrations hither, and raising the conditions of new Appropriations of Lands.[10] ___

He has obstructed the Administration of Justice, by refusing his Assent to Laws for establishing Judiciary powers.[11] ___

---

[9] This entry, along with the three previous entries, is expressing a core grievance: that by dissolving and manipulating legislatures, the King has deliberately eroded colonial peoples' right to govern themselves. At stake is a core democratic principle—that legitimate government arises solely from the consent and representation of the governed.

[10] Here George III is accused of blocking legislation that allowed the colonies to naturalize foreigners and further populate their states—for example, North Carolina's law exempting European immigrants from taxes for four years. The colonies saw this as an attempt to stifle their growth: many of them sought new independent-minded settlers to cultivate more land and bolster their economic development.

[11] This grievance refers to colonial legislatures' attempts to establish independent courts, which George III obstructed by withholding assent. It reflects early American thinking that concentrated power is a threat to liberty—and anticipates the separation of executive, legislative and judicial powers that would later appear in the Constitution.

He has made Judges dependent on his Will alone, for the tenure of their offices, and the amount and payment of their salaries. ——

He has erected a multitude of New Offices, and sent hither swarms of Officers to harrass our people, and eat out their substance.[12] ——

He has kept among us, in times of peace, Standing Armies without the Consent of our legislatures. ——

He has affected to render the Military independent of and superior to the Civil power.[13] ——

He has combined with others to subject us to a jurisdiction foreign to our constitution, and

---

[12] "eat out their substance": to drain someone entirely of their resources and livelihood. The phrasing is intentionally dramatic, implying that the British Officers sent to enforce unfair taxation on the colonists are effectively draining them of their economic vitality.

[13] Most of the grievances, like this one, are alluding to specific injustices, even when those are not outlined in detail. Sometimes the grievances relate to events in specific colonies, other times they are broader. In this case, the grievance refers to the Mutiny Acts passed annually in the British Parliament since 1765. These permitted British troops to be stationed in the colonies without their consent, subordinating colonial authority to British military control.

unacknowledged by our laws; giving his Assent to their Acts of pretended Legislation: ___

For Quartering large bodies of armed troops among us:[14] ___

For protecting them, by a mock Trial, from punishment for any Murders which they should commit on the Inhabitants of these States: ___

For cutting off our Trade with all parts of the world: ___

For imposing Taxes on us without our Consent: ___

For depriving us in many cases, of the benefits of Trial by Jury: ___

For transporting us beyond Seas to be tried for pretended offences: ___

For abolishing the free System of English Laws in a neighbouring Province, establishing therein an

---

[14] "Quartering": This refers to the 1765 Quartering Act, expanded in 1774 as part of the Coercive Acts. These laws required colonies to provide housing, food, and other supplies to British soldiers stationed in their territories—even in peacetime, and at the colonies' own expense.

Arbitrary government, and enlarging its Boundaries so as to render it at once an example and fit instrument for introducing the same absolute rule into these Colonies:[15] ___

For taking away our Charters, abolishing our most valuable Laws, and altering fundamentally the Forms of our Governments: ___

For suspending our own Legislatures, and declaring themselves invested with power to legislate for us in all cases whatsoever.

He has abdicated Government here, by declaring us out of his Protection and waging War against us. ___

He has plundered our seas, ravaged our Coasts, burnt our towns, and destroyed the lives of our people. ___

---

[15] A reference to the Quebec Act of 1774, through which Britain was governing newly-acquired Quebec—taken from France at the end of the French and Indian War in 1763. The Act extended Quebec's borders southward into the Ohio Valley, just west of several of the 13 colonies (see Figure 3). It also preserved French civil law, and allowed rule by royal appointment instead of a representative assembly. The 13 colonies feared this set a precedent for arbitrary government, undermining English legal traditions in a neighbouring territory that was now under British rule.

He is at this time transporting large Armies of foreign Mercenaries to compleat the works of death, desolation and tyranny, already begun with circumstances of Cruelty & perfidy[16] scarcely paralleled in the most barbarous ages, and totally unworthy the Head of a civilized nation. ___

He has constrained our fellow Citizens taken Captive on the high Seas to bear Arms against their Country, to become the executioners of their friends and Brethren, or to fall themselves by their Hands.[17] ___

He has excited domestic insurrections amongst us, and has endeavoured to bring on the inhabitants of our frontiers, the merciless Indian Savages,[18] whose

---

[16] perfidy: treachery, disloyalty

[17] This refers to the British wartime practice of conscripting captured colonial sailors into the Royal Navy. The phrase "or to fall themselves by their Hands" possibly conveys the anguish of being killed by fellow colonists in battle, or perhaps even choosing death over a life of servitude.

[18] This grievance reflects wartime fears, racial prejudice, and exaggerated perceptions among colonial leaders in 1776. The claim that "all men are created equal" was not extended to Native Americans defending their own lands, often with tactics similar to those of colonial forces. Nor was it applied to enslaved people. The charge that the King "excited domestic insurrections" likely refers to a proclamation by Lord Dunmore in 1775, offering freedom to enslaved people—if they joined the British army. Other than this, the Declaration makes no mention of slavery.

known rule of warfare, is an undistinguished destruction of all ages, sexes and conditions.

In every stage of these Oppressions We[19] have Petitioned for Redress in the most humble terms:

Our repeated Petitions have been answered only by repeated injury. A Prince,[20] whose character is thus marked by every act which may define a Tyrant, is unfit to be the ruler of a free people.

Nor have We been wanting in attentions to our Brittish brethren.[21] We have warned them from time to time of attempts by their legislature to

---

19 The final section of the Declaration begins. The focus now is on appeals made, and actions now being taken, by the 13 united States. "We" appears for the first time since the famous second sentence. It will be used six more times, as the text moves towards its conclusion and the signers fully implicate themselves in their historic decision.

20 "A Prince": In the 18th-century, "Prince" was a common generic term for a monarch or ruler with sovereign (sometimes absolute) power. The word appears in the writings of political philosophers such as Niccolò Machiavelli (*The Prince,* 1532), John Locke (*Two Treatises of Government,* 1689), and Baron de Montesquieu (*The Spirit of the Laws,* 1748). Here it is being used knowingly, appealing to the expected readership's familiarity with these and other thinkers' writing.

21 "our Brittish brethren": A clear acknowledgement that the colonies have, until this pivotal moment, considered themselves to be British.

extend an unwarrantable jurisdiction over us. We have reminded them of the circumstances of our emigration and settlement here. We have appealed to their native justice and magnanimity, and we have conjured them by the ties of our common kindred to disavow these usurpations, which, would inevitably interrupt our connections and correspondence.

They too have been deaf to the voice of justice and of consanguinity.[22] We must, therefore, acquiesce in the necessity,[23] which denounces our Separation, and hold them, as we hold the rest of mankind, Enemies in War, in Peace Friends. ___

We, therefore, the Representatives of the united States of America,[24] in General Congress, Assembled, appealing to the Supreme

---

22 consanguinity: kinship, shared ancestry

23 "acquiesce in the necessity": This phrase echoes an earlier rhetorical point (page 3, footnotes 4 & 5)—that the colonies are left with no choice but to separate from Britain. They are not to blame for these circumstances; they "acquiesce" in that they yield/submit to this unavoidable course of action.

24 "united States of America": The lowercase "u" suggests that, in making this Declaration, the colonies saw themselves as a collective of distinct political entities, joined in the common cause of asserting their individual Statehood. At this stage, "united" does not yet refer to a clear national identity like that of the modern USA (see also footnote 26).

Judge of the world[25] for the rectitude of our intentions, do, in the Name, and by Authority of the good People of these Colonies, solemnly publish and declare, That these United Colonies are, and of Right ought to be Free and Independent States;[26] that they are Absolved from all Allegiance to the British Crown, and that all political connection between them and the State of Great Britain, is and ought to be totally dissolved;[27] and that as Free and Independent States, they have full Power to levy War, conclude Peace, contract Alliances, establish Commerce,

---

[25] "appealing to the Supreme Judge of the world": This is the document's third reference to God, and He is now given a distinctly legal title—Judge. The appeal is no longer to the British Crown but to the highest authority of all. This suggests a legal case, with "the rectitude of our intentions" being the key argument for the justice of the colonies' cause.

[26] "these United Colonies are, and of Right ought to be Free and Independent States": There is a paradox in this phrasing —the colonies are "United" as if they are one entity, yet each claims to be "Independent", suggesting full, equal, individual sovereignty. This duality anticipates how the States would later understand their new relationship when they began drafting the Articles of Confederation in 1777.

[27] "is and ought to be totally dissolved": The verb tenses in this phrase demonstrate that the colonies are not asking for permission to break from Great Britain. By placing "is" first, the Declaration presents independence as a *fait accompli*, with this document serving to notify that fact to the world.

and to do all other Acts and Things which Independent States may of right do. ———

And for the support of this Declaration, with a firm reliance on the protection of divine Providence, we mutually pledge to each other our Lives,[28] our Fortunes and our sacred Honor.[29]

★★

[28] "we mutually pledge to each other our Lives…": The closing pledge underscores the signers' full commitment to independence, regardless of the consequences. The wording is likely a deliberate signal to Great Britain, stressing the signers' willingness to sacrifice everything. Notably, they pledge their Lives first: even if conflict with Britain now escalates on account of their decision, they fully accept all the associated risks, including death.

[29] The signatures of the 56 signers appear immediately after this closing sentence. John Hancock (MA), president of the Second Continental Congress, signs first.

The Story of 1776

In the 1760s and 1770s, Britain's escalating dominance of its American colonies – imposing taxes without any corresponding democratic representation for them in the British Parliament – was met with widespread protest and dissent. Colonial indignation over legislation such as the 1765 Stamp Act and the 1774 Coercive Acts sparked confrontation. What initially began as relatively peaceful resistance – such as the Boston Tea Party in December 1773 – eventually turned violent. In April 1775 at Lexington and Concord (MA), blood was shed for the first time in battles between colonial militias and the British regular army. This was the first exchange of the Revolutionary War, now remembered as "the shot heard around the world."

In late 1774, the colonies had already sought reconciliation with Britain through a coordinated body: the First Continental Congress. But their appeals were ignored by the mother country, and King George III ordered further military escalation. In response, representatives from the colonies convened again in May 1775 for the Second Continental Congress. Delegates began organizing further resistance by establishing a Continental Army. They discussed how the colonies' rights could be restored and whether their relationship to Britain might need to be redefined.

In 1775, most colonists – elite and ordinary people alike – still saw themselves as loyal British subjects. But the meaning of "American" was starting to change: evolving from a geographical label within the British Empire into a distinct, independent identity.

The Road to Declaration: America Rises, 1763–1775

For well over a century after the Pilgrims landed at Plymouth in 1620, Great Britain typically treated its American colonies with "salutary neglect"—a phrase first used by Parliamentarian Edmund Burke in 1775 to describe the long relationship, rooted in free trade and minimal interference. This began to change in the mid-18th century, when Britain's mounting war debt prompted it to levy new taxes on the prosperous, largely self-governing colonies.

1754–1763 — The French and Indian War pits Great Britain and its American colonies against France and its Native American allies, in a long conflict for control of territory and trade in the continent's northeast. Britain emerges victorious, but is now heavily in debt. New taxes and tighter controls on the American colonies will follow, leading to immediate discontent. The war has also started to affect the mindset of some colonists—George Washington, a young colonel from Virginia who willingly fought for King and country but has been overlooked for promotion, complains that American servicemen are treated

Figure 2: George Washington, a colonel fighting for Britain in the French and Indian War

differently than their British brethren: "We can't conceive, that being Americans should deprive us of the benefits of British Subjects; nor lessen our claim to preferment ..."[30]

April 1764 — In an attempt to raise revenue after the crippling expense of the French and Indian War, the British Parliament enacts the Sugar Act, imposing duties on molasses, sugar and other items imported into the American colonies. Colonists soon protest that this is "taxation without representation", since they have no voice in the British Parliament themselves.

March 22, 1765 — Parliament passes the Stamp Act, requiring colonists to buy stamped paper to print newspapers, court filings, and more. These are an unprecedented internal direct tax on daily life. The backlash is immediate: colonial printers denounce it; merchants organize boycotts of British goods; mobs burn effigies of tax collectors.

Figure 3:
The Stamp Act required printers to use stamped paper from the British government. Price: one penny per sheet.

October 1765 — Delegates from nine colonies gather in New York for the Stamp Act Congress. They adopt the Declaration of Rights and Grievances, formally asserting that only colonial legislatures have the right to tax colonial people. The Declaration is the first coordinated intercolonial protest, and marks the start of organized and united rebellion.

March 18, 1766 — Under pressure from colonial boycotts and economic disruption, Parliament repeals the unpopular Stamp Act. But to be certain of reasserting its authority, it immediately passes the Declaratory Act, claiming the right to legislate for the colonies "in all cases whatsoever." Though the repeal feels like a colonial victory, the Declaratory Act demonstrates Britain's

30 Letter to Robert Dinwiddie, Lieutenant Governor of Virginia, March 10, 1757

insistence on its power over the American colonies, signaling a broader conflict ahead.

June–July 1767 — The Townshend Acts impose duties on widely-used goods imported by the colonies, such as glass, paper, paint, and tea. Colonial legislatures are bypassed and revenue is partly used to pay royal officials. Colonists immediately protest and organize boycotts, especially in major ports, eventually leading to a partial repeal. Nevertheless, the British Parliament retains duties on tea in a deliberate show of authority—it aims to continue taxing the colonies one way or another.

March 5, 1770 — British soldiers open fire on an agitated crowd during a protest in Boston, killing five colonists in what becomes known as the Boston Massacre. The city has been occupied since late 1768, with British troops patrolling the streets to enforce customs duties and maintain order amid growing unrest. The day after the Massacre, Samuel Adams, a leading local politician, confronts the acting British governor, Thomas Hutchinson, and demands that British troops withdraw from the city. Hutchinson reluctantly agrees. The avoidable deaths of ordinary citizens become symbolic of British tyranny, and the King's troops are seen as an occupying, oppressive army.

Figure 4:
Samuel Adams pointing to the charter and seal of Massachusetts

May–December 1773 — In May, the Tea Act grants the East India Company (founded in England in 1600 but struggling financially) exclusive rights to ship tea directly to North America from the Far East. This new law bypasses colonial merchants—and smugglers—and is an unexpected change in how this popular staple, enjoyed by all social classes, is brought to the continent.

Additionally, importation duties need to be paid, based on the Townshend Acts. Though these taxes are modest, once again it is the principle of taxation without representation that leads to specific and dramatic colonial opposition. On a cold December night in Boston, several dozen men board East India Company ships anchored in the harbor, and proceed to dump 342 chests of tea overboard into the water. The protesters—mostly from the colonial rebel group the Sons of Liberty, some dressed as Mohawk Native Americans—signal that they would rather see the tea sink to the bottom of the harbor than pay a tax for the privilege of drinking it.

Figure 5:
The Boston Tea Party, December 16, 1773

The term "Tea Party" is not used at the time to describe the protest—this would emerge later, capturing the raucousness of this non-violent, party-style demonstration. But word of the unusual protest soon spreads nonetheless, further uniting colonists in their contempt for the string of new laws being imposed on them.

March–June 1774 — Britain reacts swiftly to the Boston protest: it retaliates with the officially named "Coercive Acts".

Among these, the Boston Port Act closes Boston Harbor until the loss of tea is repaid; the Massachusetts Government Act replaces locally elected officials with royal appointees; the Quartering Act expands Britain's power to require the colonies to house its soldiers. The colonies view these as an onerous assault on their liberties, and call them the "Intolerable Acts". The Acts also mark a shift in British legislation—toward greater political control and collective punishment.

September 5, 1774 — The colonies convene a Continental Congress in Philadelphia to discuss the growing crisis; in attendance at this first pan-colonial gathering are leaders from 12 colonies. The Congress agrees the first united stance against Britain in response to the Intolerable Acts: a boycott of British goods, and issuance of a "Declaration and Resolves", outlining the colonies' rights and their objections to the Acts. Importantly, Congress also establishes committees to oversee decisions on points of agreement—these are the first administrative bodies of what will become a new continental bureaucracy; initially it is named the Continental Association.

March 23, 1775 — Patrick Henry, a fiery Virginia lawyer and delegate to the First Continental Congress, delivers his famous "Give me liberty, or give me death!" speech at Saint John's Church, Richmond, where delegates to Virginia's Second Convention have gathered to debate the crisis. Some of the colony's most prominent men are in attendance: George Washington, Thomas Jefferson, and Richard Henry Lee among them.

Figure 6:
Patrick Henry's speech at the Second Virginia Convention, 1775

Patrick Henry urges immediate preparation for conflict with Britain, insisting that the colonies can no longer hope for reconciliation. After a passionate debate both for and against, the Convention adopts Henry's resolution on organizing, equipping, and training Virginia's militia—marking a decisive step toward armed resistance.

April 19, 1775 — British troops in Massachusetts march on Lexington and Concord, following reports that colonial militias are stockpiling arms in anticipation of rebellion. A Boston silversmith, Paul Revere, becomes aware of British plans and rides ahead with others to warn that the British are coming. In response, colonial "Minute Men"—civilian soldiers trained to mobilize at a moment's notice—assemble in anticipation. At Lexington, a brief skirmish kills several militia men. In a larger confrontation at Concord's North Bridge the colonists repel the British troops, forcing their retreat to Boston. At the day's end, dozens are dead on both sides.

Figure 7:
Concorde's Old North Bridge

These engagements mark the outbreak of the Revolutionary War. Armed opposition to British rule has begun—and with a small but significant victory for the colonial cause.

May 10, 1775 — The Second Continental Congress convenes in Philadelphia, with delegates from twelve colonies initially present (Georgia joins in July). It begins to function like a proto-national government, taking decisive steps toward war: the Continental Army is soon established and George Washington is appointed Commander-in-Chief. Congress also authorizes the printing of paper currency to fund the war effort.

Also on May 10, American forces led by farmer-turned-soldier Ethan Allen, capture Fort Ticonderoga in northern New York,

Figure 8:
Ethan Allen demanding the surrender of Fort Ticonderoga

an early military gain for the colonies. Its artillery is later transported by Henry Knox to Boston, bolstering Washington's siege of the city (see page 27).

June 17, 1775 — After the successes of the battles of Lexington and Concord, colonial militia sought to contain the British in Boston, surrounding the city and fortifying high ground overlooking the harbor. In June, they hastily entrenched on Breed's Hill. To break the siege, British forces ferried troops across the Charles River and launched frontal assaults up the slope. They eventually drove the colonist troops from their position, but only after sustaining heavy casualties—over 1,000 dead and wounded, compared to around 400 on the colonial side. Technically this was a British victory, but the scale of their losses showed that the colonial militia could stand up to the world's most powerful professional army. The engagement is remembered as the Battle of Bunker Hill, named for the larger neighboring hill that was the original objective.

Figure 9:
King George III

July 5, 1775 — Congress sends the Olive Branch Petition to King George III, pleading for his protection from Parliament's repeated overreach. The Petition affirms the colonies' sense of loyalty and identity with the mother country, declaring that they are "connected with Great Britain by the strongest ties, deploring every event that tends in any degree to weaken them." The Petition is replete with similarly effusive assertions: "We ever have been, and shall be, while blessed with the opportunity, zealous to demonstrate our loyalty and affection." There are no indications in the text of a desire for independence. But the Petition may be a strategic, final appeal: its refusal would demonstrate Britain's complete disregard for the colonies' grievances, giving them just cause to move decisively toward self-determination.

August 23, 1775 — The King refuses to receive the Petition and issues the Proclamation of Rebellion. The opening line states: "... many of Our Subjects in divers Parts of Our Colonies and Plantations in North America, misled by dangerous and ill-designing Men ... have at length proceeded to an open and avowed Rebellion ... traitorously preparing, ordering, and levying War against Us ...". The rest of the 400-word text is succinct but uncompromising in its message, leaving little room for reconciliation: "... all our Officers, civil and military, are obliged to exert their utmost Endeavours to suppress such Rebellion, and to bring the Traitors to Justice ..."

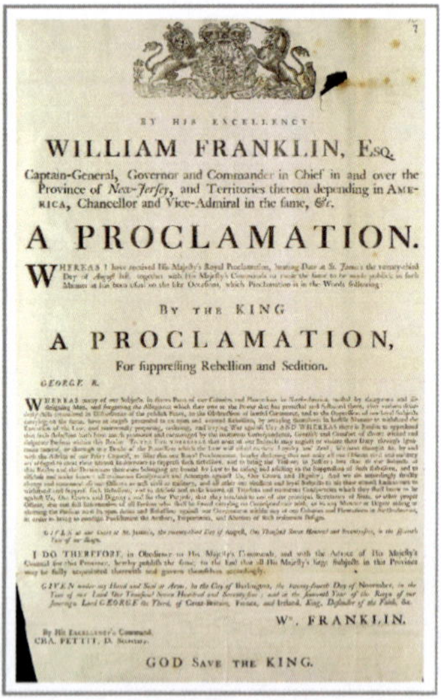
BY HIS EXCELLENCY

WILLIAM FRANKLIN, Esq.

Captain-General, Governor and Commander in Chief in and over the Province of *New-Jersey*, and Territories thereon depending in AMERICA, Chancellor and Vice-Admiral in the same, *&c.*

A PROCLAMATION.

WHEREAS I have received His Majesty's Royal Proclamation, bearing Date at St. *James's* the twenty-third Day of *August* last, together with His Majesty's Commands to cause the same to be made publick in such Manner as has been usual on the like Occasions, which Proclamation is in the Words following:

BY THE KING

A PROCLAMATION,

For suppressing Rebellion and Sedition.

GEORGE R.

[illegible]

[illegible]

I DO THEREFORE, [illegible]

[illegible]

W^m. FRANKLIN.

By His EXCELLENCY'S Command.
CHA. PETTIT, D. Secretary.

GOD SAVE THE KING.

Figure 10:
A copy of the Proclamation of Rebellion as printed and distributed by William Franklin, the loyalist Governor of New Jersey, in November 1775

The Proclamation reaches the colonies in the fall of 1775; its stark content does not intimidate the most radical colonial leaders. Calls for independence grow even louder as a tumultuous year draws to a close.

The Turning Point: America Decides, 1776

The year 1776 begins with the publication of a pamphlet that is widely read throughout the colonies, making the case for full American independence. Meanwhile, delegates to the Second Continental Congress continue their work, organizing resistance and debating the colonies' futures. Many are now arguing for a complete break from Britain—but there is no unanimous consensus yet that this is desirable or necessary.

January to March: Uncertainty

January 10, 1776 — Thomas Paine, an English writer based in Philadelphia, publishes *Common Sense*, a pamphlet advocating full independence for the colonies. It purportedly sells more than 100,000 copies and begins to sway public opinion. Paine's outspoken arguments help to radicalize the colonial cause. His assessment is blunt: "there is something very absurd, in supposing a continent to be perpetually governed by an island."

Figure 11: Thomas Paine

February 1776 — Paine's ideas are not universally well received, however, nor indeed universally read. At this stage in the Second Continental Congress, Massachusetts is the most vociferous of the four New England colonies (CT, MA,

NH, RI) in pushing for independence. Recalling the Battles of Lexington, Concord, and Bunker Hill on its soil, its

Figure 12: Eastern North America in 1776 – The 13 British colonies that would unite to declare independence from Britain are New Hampshire (NH), Massachusetts (MA), Rhode Island (RI), Connecticut (CT), New York (NY), New Jersey (NJ), Pennsylvania (PA), Delaware (DE), Maryland (MD), Virginia (VA), North Carolina (NC), South Carolina (SC), Georgia (GA).

delegates view British military escalation as ominous and beyond the point of no return. Most of the five Middle Colonies (commonly defined as DE, MD, NJ, NY, PA) are hesitant or opposed to outright independence. Their economies are more intertwined with British trade, and their merchant and Quaker elites favor reconciliation. The Southern Colonies (GA, NC, SC, VA) are split. Virginia is emerging as a pro-independence colony: it is populous, wealthy, and has assertive leadership. But South Carolina and Georgia remain wary, fearing that a break from Britain could trigger slave revolts and threaten their plantation economies.

Early March, 1776 — Opinion remains divided and only the more radical delegates, such as John Adams (MA), Thomas Jefferson (VA), and Richard Henry Lee (VA), advocate for a clean break from Britain. In the opposite camp, delegates like John Dickinson (PA) urge negotiation and reconciliation with the mother country. He reflects a widely-held view: that separation could be ruinous in many different ways, disconnecting the colonies from the identity, institutions, laws and culture they share with Britain.

Figure 13:
John Dickinson

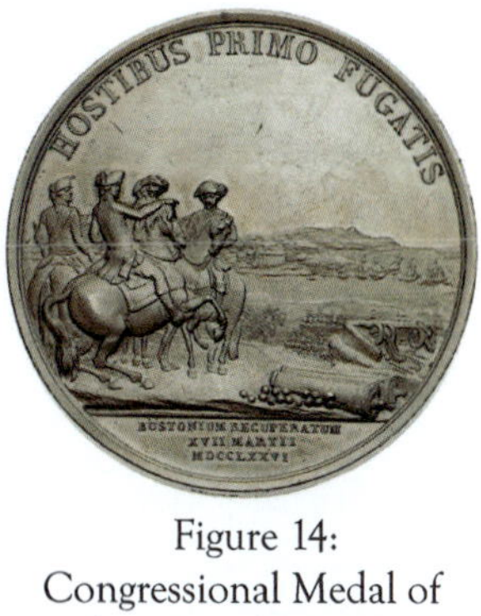

Figure 14:
Congressional Medal of Washington above Boston harbor, "With the enemy first made to flee"

March 17, 1776 — British troops retreat from Boston following a successful siege of the city by colonial forces that has lasted more than 11 months. Led by George Washington, the victory is a major boost to morale for the colonies, now united military and succeeding on the battlefield. Thousands of British troops are forced to move north to Nova Scotia.

March 23, 1776 — In an assertive and audacious move, the Continental Congress decides to authorize colonial ports to trade with the whole world, excluding Britain. For decades, British policy had dictated that the colonies could only trade with the mother country, ensuring a captive market for British goods, and a cheap source of raw materials flowing the other way. This is now a major step towards commercial independence.

April to June: Progress

April 12, 1776 — North Carolina's Provincial Congress adopts the Halifax Resolves, after meeting in the town of the same name. These make it the first colony to authorize its delegates to vote for independence should the circumstances arise. The Resolves are bold and encourage all delegates to the Continental Congress to move to sever ties with Britain, though they fall just short of a formal proposal.

Figure 15:
The North Carolina flag commemorates the date of the Halifax Resolves

May 10, 1776 — Congress passes a resolution urging the colonies to set up new governments based on democratic principles alone. It suggests that the authority of the British Crown should be "totally suppressed". Written by John Adams, the resolution is also unequivocal about representative legitimacy: powers of government should be exerted "under the authority of the people of the colonies".

May 15, 1776 — The Fifth Virginia Convention meets at the Williamsburg Capitol to debate and agree the colony's position. Virginia has been in the vanguard of vigorous action against escalating British dominance, having already celebrated four similar conventions since 1774. These replaced royal authority and began organizing the colony's defense and revolutionary governance. At this pivotal

Figure 16:
The reconstructed
Williamsburg Capitol today

gathering, Virginia's elected delegates now unanimously vote to instruct their delegates to the Continental Congress to formally propose independence.

June 7, 1776 — Richard Henry Lee (VA) duly introduces his eponymous Lee Resolution in Philadelphia. It begins: "Resolved, That these United Colonies are, and of right ought to be, free and independent States, that they are absolved from all allegiance to the British Crown ..." Several delegates from Middle Colonies respond hesitantly: they first want to consult their home governments before confirming support.

June 11, 1776 — Congress appoints the Committee of Five to draft a potential declaration. The chosen men represent a range of colonies from north to south, and are established respected leaders: John Adams (MA), Roger Sherman (CT), Robert R. Livingston (NY), Benjamin Franklin (PA), and Thomas Jefferson (VA).

June 12–27, 1776 — Jefferson is tasked with writing the first draft of the Declaration; he sets to work at his small desk in his rented room on Market Street. The draft is copied and shared with the other four Committee members; Adams and Franklin make some important suggestions. Jefferson finalizes the draft while also performing other duties in Congress: it is an intense, draining, productive two weeks.

Figure 17:
The reconstructed
Declaration House in
Philadelphia, Thomas
Jefferson's 1776 lodgings

June 28, 1776 — The Committee of Five presents the draft Declaration of Independence to Congress, as depicted in John Trumbull's famous painting more than 40 years later. It is set aside for debate the following Monday, 1 July.

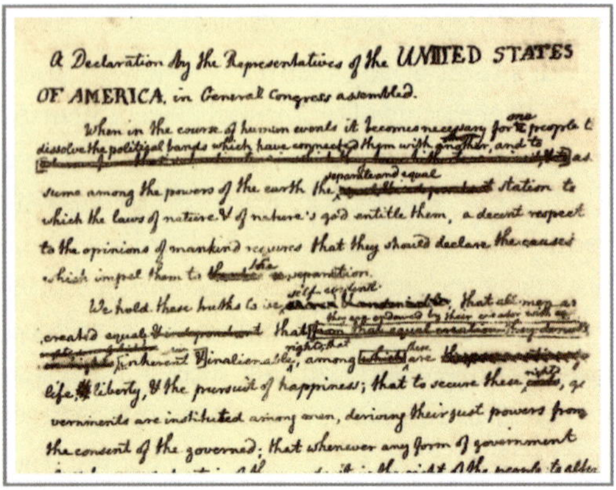
A Declaration by the Representatives of the UNITED STATES OF AMERICA, in General Congress assembled.

When in the course of human events it becomes necessary for one people to dissolve the political bands which have connected them with another, and to assume among the powers of the earth the separate and equal station to which the laws of nature & of nature's god entitle them, a decent respect to the opinions of mankind requires that they should declare the causes which impel them to the separation.

We hold these truths to be self-evident, that all men are created equal; that they are endowed by their creator with inherent & inalienable rights; that among these are life, liberty, & the pursuit of happiness; that to secure these rights, governments are instituted among men, deriving their just powers from the consent of the governed; that whenever any form of government

Figure 18: Original corrected rough draft of the Declaration of Independence, in Jefferson's hand

July: Decision

July 1, 1776 — Congress begins its formal debate on independence. Some delegates oppose the motion, notably John Dickinson (PA) and Robert Morris (PA), a wealthy merchant who abstains. South Carolina (led by Edward Rutledge) is somewhat reluctant, and the three-man Delaware delegation is split: Caesar Rodney is not currently in Philadelphia, while Thomas McKean is in favor, and George Read is against.

July 2, 1776 — Support begins to shift, with delegates from Pennsylvania and South Carolina now voting for independence. Caesar Rodney has ridden to Philadelphia overnight through a storm, arriving just in time to cast his tie-breaking vote in favor.

Figure 19: Caesar Rodney

July 2, 1776 — Congress votes to declare independence: 12 colonies support it and New York abstains. As there are no votes against, this confirms the democratic decision to separate from Great Britain. John Adams famously and incorrectly predicts that July 2 will now be remembered and celebrated as a national holiday.

July 3, 1776 — Congressional delegates carefully edit the Declaration, finessing the meaning and message of its language. About twenty-five percent of Thomas Jefferson's original text is altered or removed. Discussions on what the exact wording should be continue late in the day.

★★ July 4, 1776 ★★ — Congress adopts the final version of the Declaration of Independence. Adoption is the last formal step in making the document official, explaining the July 4 celebrations ever since. Technically the decision is not quite unanimous yet: New York continues to abstain, awaiting instructions from its Provincial Congress.

Figure 20:
The Assembly Room at Independence Hall, Philadelphia, where the engrossed Declaration was signed, beginning 2 August 1776

Evening, July 4, 1776 — The Philadelphia printer John Dunlap typesets and prints copies of the Declaration for urgent distribution to colonial authorities and military leaders. These Dunlap broadsides are the first public copies of the single-sided document. Newspapers throughout America soon receive the historic news and start printing their own verbatim copies. Public readings are held in town squares, and word of the momentous decision soon starts to spread.

July 9, 1776 — New York's Provincial Congress approves the Declaration of Independence: the decision to cut all ties with Great Britain is now unanimous among the 13 united States.

July 19, 1776 — Congress orders that the Declaration be "engrossed" (formally handwritten) on parchment. Timothy Matlack, a clerk to the Congress, is charged with this task, on account of his attention to detail and elegant hand.

August 2, 1776 — Most delegates sign the engrossed copy of the Declaration. Some sign it later, though a few never sign. Either way, after their unanimous adoption of the text, all 13 States are now fully committed to this historic decision.

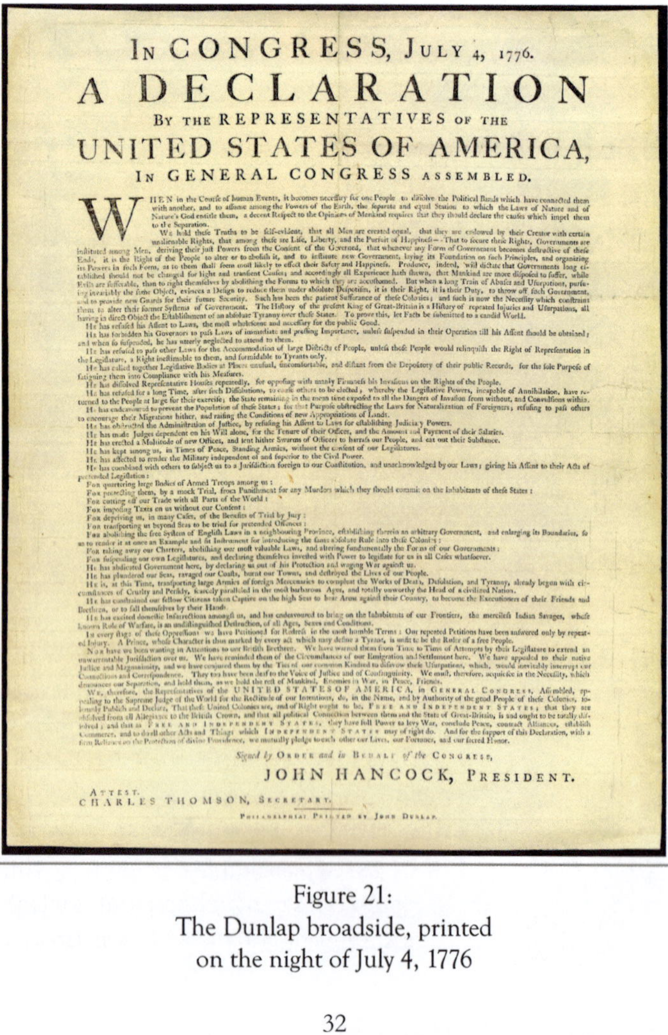

IN CONGRESS, JULY 4, 1776.

A DECLARATION

BY THE REPRESENTATIVES OF THE

UNITED STATES OF AMERICA,

IN GENERAL CONGRESS ASSEMBLED.

WHEN in the Course of human Events, it becomes necessary for one People to dissolve the Political Bands which have connected them with another, and to assume among the Powers of the Earth, the separate and equal Station to which the Laws of Nature and of Nature's God entitle them, a decent Respect to the Opinions of Mankind requires that they should declare the causes which impel them to the Separation.

We hold these Truths to be self-evident, that all Men are created equal, that they are endowed by their Creator with certain unalienable Rights, that among these are Life, Liberty, and the Pursuit of Happiness—That to secure these Rights, Governments are instituted among Men, deriving their just Powers from the Consent of the Governed, that whenever any Form of Government becomes destructive of these Ends, it is the Right of the People to alter or to abolish it, and to institute new Government, laying its Foundation on such Principles, and organizing its Powers in such Form, as to them shall seem most likely to effect their Safety and Happiness. Prudence, indeed, will dictate that Governments long established should not be changed for light and transient Causes; and accordingly all Experience hath shewn, that Mankind are more disposed to suffer, while Evils are sufferable, than to right themselves by abolishing the Forms to which they are accustomed. But when a long Train of Abuses and Usurpations, pursuing invariably the same Object, evinces a Design to reduce them under absolute Despotism, it is their Right, it is their Duty, to throw off such Government, and to provide new Guards for their future Security. Such has been the patient Sufferance of these Colonies; and such is now the Necessity which constrains them to alter their former Systems of Government. The History of the present King of Great-Britain is a History of repeated Injuries and Usurpations, all having in direct Object the Establishment of an absolute Tyranny over these States. To prove this, let Facts be submitted to a candid World.

He has refused his Assent to Laws, the most wholesome and necessary for the public Good.

He has forbidden his Governors to pass Laws of immediate and pressing Importance, unless suspended in their Operation till his Assent should be obtained; and when so suspended, he has utterly neglected to attend to them.

He has refused to pass other Laws for the Accommodation of large Districts of People, unless those People would relinquish the Right of Representation in the Legislature, a Right inestimable to them, and formidable to Tyrants only.

He has called together Legislative Bodies at Places unusual, uncomfortable, and distant from the Depository of their public Records, for the sole Purpose of fatiguing them into Compliance with his Measures.

He has dissolved Representative Houses repeatedly, for opposing with manly Firmness his Invasions on the Rights of the People.

He has refused for a long Time, after such Dissolutions, to cause others to be elected; whereby the Legislative Powers, incapable of Annihilation, have returned to the People at large for their exercise; the State remaining in the mean time exposed to all the Dangers of Invasion from without, and Convulsions within.

He has endeavoured to prevent the Population of these States; for that Purpose obstructing the Laws for Naturalization of Foreigners; refusing to pass others to encourage their Migrations hither, and raising the Conditions of new Appropriations of Lands.

He has obstructed the Administration of Justice, by refusing his Assent to Laws for establishing Judiciary Powers.

He has made Judges dependent on his Will alone, for the Tenure of their Offices, and the Amount and Payment of their Salaries.

He has erected a Multitude of new Offices, and sent hither Swarms of Officers to harrass our People, and eat out their Substance.

He has kept among us, in Times of Peace, Standing Armies, without the consent of our Legislatures.

He has affected to render the Military independent of and superior to the Civil Power.

He has combined with others to subject us to a Jurisdiction foreign to our Constitution, and unacknowledged by our Laws; giving his Assent to their Acts of pretended Legislation:

For quartering large Bodies of Armed Troops among us:

For protecting them, by a mock Trial, from Punishment for any Murders which they should commit on the Inhabitants of these States:

For cutting off our Trade with all Parts of the World:

For imposing Taxes on us without our Consent:

For depriving us, in many Cases, of the Benefits of Trial by Jury:

For transporting us beyond Seas to be tried for pretended Offences:

For abolishing the free System of English Laws in a neighbouring Province, establishing therein an arbitrary Government, and enlarging its Boundaries, so as to render it at once an Example and fit Instrument for introducing the same absolute Rule into these Colonies:

For taking away our Charters, abolishing our most valuable Laws, and altering fundamentally the Forms of our Governments:

For suspending our own Legislatures, and declaring themselves invested with Power to legislate for us in all Cases whatsoever.

He has abdicated Government here, by declaring us out of his Protection and waging War against us.

He has plundered our Seas, ravaged our Coasts, burnt our Towns, and destroyed the Lives of our People.

He is, at this Time, transporting large Armies of foreign Mercenaries to compleat the Works of Death, Desolation, and Tyranny, already begun with circumstances of Cruelty and Perfidy, scarcely paralleled in the most barbarous Ages, and totally unworthy the Head of a civilized Nation.

He has constrained our fellow Citizens taken Captive on the high Seas to bear Arms against their Country, to become the Executioners of their Friends and Brethren, or to fall themselves by their Hands.

He has excited domestic Insurrections amongst us, and has endeavoured to bring on the Inhabitants of our Frontiers, the merciless Indian Savages, whose known Rule of Warfare, is an undistinguished Destruction, of all Ages, Sexes and Conditions.

In every stage of these Oppressions we have Petitioned for Redress in the most humble Terms: Our repeated Petitions have been answered only by repeated Injury. A Prince, whose Character is thus marked by every act which may define a Tyrant, is unfit to be the Ruler of a free People.

Nor have we been wanting in Attentions to our British Brethren. We have warned them from Time to Time of Attempts by their Legislature to extend an unwarrantable Jurisdiction over us. We have reminded them of the Circumstances of our Emigration and Settlement here. We have appealed to their native Justice and Magnanimity, and we have conjured them by the Ties of our common Kindred to disavow these Usurpations, which, would inevitably interrupt our Connections and Correspondence. They too have been deaf to the Voice of Justice and of Consanguinity. We must, therefore, acquiesce in the Necessity, which denounces our Separation, and hold them, as we hold the rest of Mankind, Enemies in War, in Peace, Friends.

We, therefore, the Representatives of the UNITED STATES OF AMERICA, in GENERAL CONGRESS, Assembled, appealing to the Supreme Judge of the World for the Rectitude of our Intentions, do, in the Name, and by Authority of the good People of these Colonies, solemnly Publish and Declare, That these United Colonies are, and of Right ought to be, FREE AND INDEPENDENT STATES; that they are absolved from all Allegiance to the British Crown, and that all political Connection between them and the State of Great-Britain, is and ought to be totally dissolved; and that as FREE AND INDEPENDENT STATES, they have full Power to levy War, conclude Peace, contract Alliances, establish Commerce, and to do all other Acts and Things which INDEPENDENT STATES may of right do. And for the support of this Declaration, with a firm Reliance on the Protection of divine Providence, we mutually pledge to each other our Lives, our Fortunes, and our sacred Honor.

Signed by ORDER *and in* BEHALF *of the* CONGRESS,

JOHN HANCOCK, PRESIDENT.

ATTEST.
CHARLES THOMSON, SECRETARY.

PHILADELPHIA: PRINTED BY JOHN DUNLAP.

Figure 21:
The Dunlap broadside, printed
on the night of July 4, 1776

The 56 Signers

As colonial delegates gathered for the Second Continental Congress in Philadelphia beginning May 10, 1775, few would have predicted that just over one year later, 56 attendees would declare the 13 colonies' relationship with Great Britain null and void. All of the delegates were white men and many had similar backgrounds as lawyers and merchants; they were accustomed to privilege and were confident operators within the British system. Unsurprisingly then, some still held out hope for reconciliation with the mother country. But with Britain showing no willingness to discuss the colonies' grievances, and military conflict escalating, events on the ground over the next 14 months would push Congress toward the most radical of decisions.

Unilaterally declaring independence from Britain was the boldest move imaginable, and took the British elite by surprise. Both Parliament and the King saw the Declaration as an impudent act of treason, punishable by death. Conflict with Britain had already been escalating for many months, and the British Army and Navy – on paper, far superior to the nascent Continental Army – would now be called on to act decisively and crush the rebellion. Nevertheless, on July 4, 1776, the representatives of the thirteen colonies unequivocally declared their liberty, fully expecting a long fight ahead to secure it. All necessary signatures were then signed on the Declaration's official parchment from 2 August.

In a letter to John Adams many years later, signer Benjamin Rush recalled the tension of the moment: "Do you recollect the pensive and awful silence which pervaded the house when we were called up, one after another, to the table of the president of Congress, to subscribe what was believed by many at that time to be our own death warrants?"

Making a Nation: Five Key Movers

This section profiles five of the most influential men who signed the Declaration of Independence—though to be clear, the signatures of the other 51 delegates were equally important. All 56 signers were crucial to demonstrating the combined will and certitude of the 13 States, confirming the momentous and unanimous decision of July 4, 1776.

John Adams
Born 1735, Braintree, MA
Lawyer, Aged 40
Representing Massachusetts

John Adams was a Harvard-educated lawyer who had come to prominence in his home state when he defended British soldiers after the 1770 Boston Massacre—demonstrating his deep commitment to fair trials and the judicial process. At the Second Continental Congress he soon emerged as a leading radical, calling for complete independence from Great Britain. Intellectually brilliant but often blunt, he nevertheless showed sufficient restraint in the crucial weeks of 1776 to work to build consensus. Adams was appointed to the Committee of Five to write the Declaration, but suggested that Thomas Jefferson would be a more eloquent writer of the first draft.

Many of the letters he sent from Congress to his beloved wife, Abigail, survive to this day. On July 3, he wrote her:

> *"I am well aware of the Toil and Blood and Treasure, that it will cost Us to maintain this Declaration and support and defend these States.—Yet through all the Gloom I can see the Rays of ravishing Light and Glory."*

Adams was prescient in foreseeing the sacrifices that lay ahead, and would live long enough to witness the emergence of the USA as a firmly-established sovereign nation. He would also contribute further: more than 20 years after signing the Declaration, he served as second president of the United States (1797–1801), having already served as its first vice president under George Washington.

He passed away aged 90, on July 4, 1826—exactly 50 years after the Declaration of Independence was adopted.

Benjamin Franklin
Born 1707, Boston, MA
Printer/Statesman, Aged 70
Representing Pennsylvania

The oldest signer of the Declaration of Independence, Benjamin Franklin was a largely self-educated polymath. Already an entrepreneur and printer by his early 20s, he would later turn his formidable mind to science. He famously flew a kite in a thunderstorm to demonstrate that lightning is electrical in nature, and then invented the lightning rod. He also invented bifocal glasses and a musical instrument, the glass harmonica.

Franklin was a civic leader too, founding the American Philosophical Society in 1743 to promote scholarly exchange. His growing reputation throughout the colonies and his networking skills then led him to become an international statesman. Between 1757 and 1774 he spent much of his time in London, representing the interests of Pennsylvania and other colonies. While there in 1766, he contributed to the repeal of the Stamp Act, testifying at the House of Commons with brilliant and compelling arguments.

Returning to Pennsylvania in May 1775 with an elevated reputation, Franklin was quickly appointed as a delegate to the Second Continental Congress. He soon proposed his Articles of Confederation and Perpetual Union, an early blueprint for colonial unity. These foreshadowed the later Articles of Confederation that the States eventually agreed to in 1781, setting them on the path to becoming one nation.

In the summer of 1776, Franklin helped turn Pennsylvania in favor of independence. As an admired elder statesman, he lent credibility to the case for declaration when his colony was not yet fully committed. He went on to serve as Minister to France during the rest of the war, securing military and financial aid that would be crucial to the eventual American victory.

When the moment came to sign the parchment of the Declaration on August 2, 1776, one delegate is said to have spoken with encouragement of the need to "hang together". Hearing this, Benjamin Franklin is reported to have responded with characteristic wit:

"We must, indeed, all hang together, or, most assuredly, we shall all hang separately."

★ ★

John Hancock
Born 1737, Braintree, MA
Merchant, Aged 39
Representing Massachusetts

In 1776, John Hancock was one of the wealthiest men in colonial America, having inherited a large mercantile empire from his uncle. A Harvard graduate, he combined business acumen with a flair for public presentation that helped him rise to prominence in Boston's political life.

When the Stamp Act came into force in 1765, Hancock did not take an immediate public stance, possibly due to his trade interests with the mother country. But as resistance to the Act grew among fellow merchants, he too became a vocal opponent. His defiance deepened after June 1768 when customs officials seized his boat, *Liberty*. They alleged that Hancock was smuggling Madeira wine into Boston without paying importation duties, required by the Townshend Acts. The charges were dropped, but this famous incident had led to riots and further inflamed tensions between colonists and the British authorities.

In October 1774, Hancock was elected president of the Massachusetts Provincial Congress, making him a prominent colonial leader as tensions with Britain grew. His subsequent election in May 1775 to the presidency of the Second Continental Congress gave him a highly visible, practical role in uniting the colonies—not least in administering Congress' committees and daily business as the war effort ramped up.

On the night of July 4, 1776, the Dunlap broadside print of the Declaration of Independence announced America's liberty to the world. Of the 56 men who would eventually sign the official parchment a month later, this first printed edition displayed Hancock's name alone: JOHN HANCOCK, PRESIDENT (see Figure 21). On August 2, he would then become the first of the 56 delegates to sign the engrossed parchment, in bold confident strokes of his quill pen.

Thomas Jefferson
Born 1743, Shadwell, VA
Lawyer/Planter, Aged 33
Representing Virginia

Thomas Jefferson was a bookish and quiet Virginian, steeped in classical learning from his time at the prestigious College of William & Mary in Williamsburg. He studied law under George Wythe, his esteemed mentor, who, 30 years later, would also sign the Declaration of Independence alongside his former pupil.

Jefferson's political awakening was slow but steady, as he became increasingly dismayed by the series of punitive Parliamentary Acts being imposed on the colonies through the 1760s and 1770s. In 1774, he emerged as a forceful voice for American rights, publishing *A Summary View of the Rights of British America*, a pamphlet arguing that the British King and Parliament had no authority over the American colonies.

In June 1776 at the Second Continental Congress, Jefferson was appointed to the Committee of Five and tasked with writing the first draft of the Declaration of Independence. Though sometimes regarded as its sole and original author, his ideas also drew on familiarity with Enlightenment works such as John Locke's *Two Treatises of Government* (see page 2). Jefferson also used wording from the Lee Resolution (see page 29), and paraphrased George Mason's Virginia Declaration of Rights, published a few weeks earlier. The famous line beginning "We hold these truths to be self-evident..." echoes Mason's phrasing, though Jefferson would refine it and build on it. Working diligently in the small room he was renting in Philadelphia, he completed the draft Declaration in two weeks, with feedback from other Committee members.

In 1779, Jefferson returned to Virginia and then helped draft the state's new constitution before serving as governor from 1779 to 1781. After the British forced him from office, he turned his attention to legislative reforms, most notably with his work on the Virginia Statute for Religious Freedom.

Jefferson's long political career peaked when he served as the third president of the United States from 1801 to 1809, succeeding John Adams. Their polarized political views had once driven them apart, but later in life they were reconciled, prompted by their mutual friend and fellow signer of the Declaration, Benjamin Rush (see page 34). They began corresponding regularly, exchanging more than 150 letters. In 1812, Jefferson wrote Adams, reminiscing about the extraordinary experiences they had shared:

> *"A letter from you calls up recollections very dear to my mind. It carries me back to the times when, beset with difficulties and dangers, we were fellow-laborers in the same cause, struggling for what is most valuable to man, his right to self-government."*

On July 4, 1826, the 50th anniversary of the Declaration of Independence, Thomas Jefferson died at his beloved Monticello estate in Virginia. Unbeknownst to him, John Adams would also pass away just a few hours later, hundreds of miles to the north in Massachusetts. Adams' final words were reportedly, "Thomas Jefferson survives me." He was mistaken.

★★

Roger Sherman
Born 1721, Newton, MA
Lawyer, Aged 55
Representing Connecticut

The modest character of Roger Sherman reflects a quiet yet pivotal contribution to the founding of the United States. Born in Massachusetts and later settling in New Milford, Connecticut, Sherman worked as a surveyor and merchant before teaching himself law.

His public career began with election to the Connecticut General Assembly. In the 1770s he opposed legislative overreach by the British Parliament, while also advocating practical solutions to the resulting disputes. In 1774 he was chosen as a delegate to the First Continental Congress, becoming a permanent delegate and contributing to the drafting of the Declaration of Independence as one of the Committee of Five.

Sherman would be continuously involved in moving the 13 States toward full union. He signed the Articles of Association (1774), the Articles of Confederation (1781), and the Constitution (1787)—the only contributor to all four of America's founding documents. At the Constitutional Convention, he proposed the Connecticut Compromise, which suggested balancing the states' voting power with two different systems: the bicameral legislature of the House of Representatives and the Senate.

Though a Puritan, Sherman also championed religious liberty. In 1783, he co-authored Connecticut's Act for Securing the Rights of Conscience, which guaranteed freedom of worship to all Christians, regardless of denomination.

Unique Stories, One Purpose

The Declaration of Independence is a unified statement of purpose and values, yet behind the names of the 56 men who signed it are a range of unique backgrounds and stories. From family ties and foreign birthplaces to millionaire signers and moral contradictions, here are some intriguing facts about the men who signed the Declaration. But first ...

A Significant Non-Signer

The most notable non-signer of the Declaration is Robert R. Livingston, a member of the Committee of Five that drafted the document. During July 1776, Livingston returned to New York City to attend to matters in his home state, and did not make the long journey back to Philadelphia to put his name to the final parchment.

Figure 22:
Robert R. Livingston

But his absence from the signing does not diminish his influence in the early history of the United States. He administered the first presidential oath of office to George Washington in New York, April 30, 1789. And as Minister to France in 1801, he played a central role in negotiating the Louisiana Purchase of 1803, resulting in the first major westward expansion of United States territory.

George Washington is sometimes incorrectly thought of as a signer of the Declaration of Independence. Although he was a standout figure in the Revolution and America's first president, in July 1776 he was not a delegate to the Second Continental Congress, but a soldier. As Commander-in-Chief of the Continental Army he was in New York, once again leading his troops against the British after the successful siege of Boston a few months earlier.

Family Ties Among the Signers

Several signers of the Declaration of Independence were related by blood or marriage—a reflection of the small, interconnected nature of the elite class across the 13 colonies.

From New York, delegate Philip Livingston was a signer of the Declaration and shared ancestral lineage with Robert R. Livingston—the man who helped draft the Declaration but did not sign it himself.

Figure 23:
Names of the New Hampshire delegates at the Memorial to the 56 Signers in Washington, D.C.

From Massachusetts, John Adams and Samuel Adams were second cousins. Both were Harvard graduates and key figures in the revolution, with Samuel Adams being more the fiery orator and grassroots organizer of the two. He has often been called "Father of the American Revolution" for his crucial role in mobilizing the public against British rule.

But the strongest family

connection was between Francis Lightfoot Lee and Richard Henry Lee: they were brothers. The Lee delegates traced their lineage to Richard Lee I, who emigrated from England in the 1640s and became a wealthy Virginia planter.

Foreign-Born Signers

Eight of the signers were born in the British Isles, a reminder that a significant number of elite Americans in 1776 were not just British subjects living in America, but British by birth. Their decision to sign the Declaration of Independence underscores the depth of their disillusionment with the mother country, despite their especially strong connections.

These eight men were Button Gwinnett (England), Francis Lewis (Wales), Robert Morris (England), James Smith (modern-day Northern Ireland), George Taylor (Ireland), Matthew Thornton (Ireland), James Wilson (Scotland), and John Witherspoon (Scotland).

Signers and Enslaved People

More than 40 of the 56 signers of the Declaration of Independence were enslavers at some point in their lives.

Figure 24:
George Washington at his Mount Vernon estate with some of the people he enslaved

These include Thomas Jefferson, who enslaved more than 600 people at his Monticello estate, and Benjamin Franklin, who kept enslaved people early in his life before turning against slavery in his final years, as president of Pennsylvania's abolitionist society. Many other revolutionary leaders also claimed ownership of enslaved people, including George Washington. Acknowledging this uncomfortable truth need not diminish the Declaration's importance or power, but is a reminder that America's founding ideals were compromised from the beginning, leaving struggles for justice and equality to future generations.

The Youngest and Oldest Signers

Edward Rutledge of South Carolina was just 26 years old when he signed the Declaration of Independence. His rapid rise among America's elite was fueled by powerful family connections in South Carolina, as well as a prestigious legal education in London.

Benjamin Franklin, aged 70, was the oldest man to sign the Declaration. He would go on to perform a variety of pivotal roles in the establishment of the United States, eventually ending his political career as one of the signers of the Constitution, just three years before his death (see page 48).

Figure 25:
Edward Rutledge House in Charleston, SC

The Last Surviving Signer

Charles Carroll of Carrollton survived all the other signers, dying in 1832 at the age of 95. He lived to see the inauguration of the 7th president of the United States in 1829, Andrew Jackson, and was still alive when the first railroads were being built in the early 1830s. At the time of his death the United States comprised 24 states with territory that reached the Mississippi River and beyond—proof if ever it was needed that the revolution he helped start was transforming the continent.

He notably added "of Carrollton" to his signature on the Declaration, possibly to distinguish himself from other men who might have the same name—and thereby ensuring there could be no doubt about who had made this bold commitment.

Figure 26:
Charles Carroll in his 90s, painted around 1830

The Wealthiest Signer?

Robert Morris may have been the wealthiest of all the signers, rivaled only by Charles Carroll. Born in 1734 in Liverpool, England, Morris emigrated to Maryland aged 13 to join his father, a tobacco exporter. He later moved to Philadelphia, where he built a vast fortune in shipping, trade, and finance. Initially very cautious about independence—to the extent that he absented himself from the final July votes to allow his Pennsylvania delegation to decide without him—by August he was nevertheless ready to sign his name on the parchment.

Figure 27:
Robert Morris

Morris became the main financier of the Revolutionary War, pledging much of his personal wealth and mobilizing his business network to supply Washington's army as best he could. His long political career saw him serve as a delegate to the Constitutional Convention in 1787; after ratification, he was elected as a Senator for Pennsylvania. Today he is remembered as the "Financier of the Revolution".

The Only Catholic Signer

Most of the 56 signers of the Declaration of Independence were of various Protestant denominations. But there was one exception—Charles Carroll (he of Carrollton) was the only Roman Catholic to sign the Declaration. This seems remarkable in an era when anti-Catholic sentiment was widespread in the colonies, rooted in both theological prejudice and political distrust. At the time, Britain was largely a Protestant country, while its major enemy in North America, France, was strongly Catholic.

But Carroll's elevated position in Maryland society afforded him a level of prestige that helped to overcome this apparent barrier. While his Catholicism may have been a source of tension, it was his vast wealth, political savvy, and associated influence that secured his presence at the Second Continental Congress.

Figure 28:
Charles Carroll House in Annapolis, MD

Signers and the Constitution

A handful of men left their signatures on both of America's most important founding documents. George Clymer, Benjamin Franklin, Robert Morris, George Read, Roger Sherman, and James Wilson all signed the Declaration of Independence in 1776 and, more than a decade later, the Constitution in 1787.

Franklin was 81 years old when he signed the Constitution, the most experienced of all the delegates and certainly one of the most consequential too. On the final day of the Constitutional

Convention, he reflected on what he saw as the guiding hand of providence in the founding of the United States:

"I have lived, Sir, a long time, and the longer I live, the more convincing proofs I see of this truth – that God governs in the affairs of men. And if a sparrow cannot fall to the ground without his notice, is it probable that an empire can rise without his aid?"

Figure 29:
The Rotunda for the Charters of Freedom, National Archives building, Washington, D.C.
The original copies of the Declaration of Independence, the U.S. Constitution, and the Bill of Rights, are all on display here.

The Full List of Signers

In alphabetical order by colony and name, these are the men who signed the Declaration of Independence, along with their ages on July 4, 1776, and their primary occupations at that time.

Samuel Huntington	44, Lawyer, Connecticut
Roger Sherman	55, Lawyer, Connecticut
William Williams	45, Merchant, Connecticut
Oliver Wolcott	50, Soldier/Politician, Connecticut
Thomas McKean	42, Lawyer, Delaware
George Read	43, Lawyer, Delaware
Caesar Rodney	47, Politician, Delaware
Button Gwinnett	41, Merchant, Georgia
Lyman Hall	52, Physician/Clergyman, Georgia
George Walton	35, Lawyer, Georgia
Charles Carroll	38, Planter, Maryland
Samuel Chase	35, Lawyer, Maryland
William Paca	35, Lawyer, Maryland
Thomas Stone	33, Lawyer, Maryland
John Adams	40, Lawyer, Massachusetts
Samuel Adams	53, Politician, Massachusetts
Elbridge Gerry	31, Merchant, Massachusetts
John Hancock	39, Merchant, Massachusetts
Robert Treat Paine	45, Lawyer, Massachusetts

Josiah Bartlett	46, Physician, New Hampshire
Matthew Thornton	62, Physician, New Hampshire
William Whipple	46, Merchant, New Hampshire
Abraham Clark	50, Lawyer, New Jersey
John Hart	65, Landowner, New Jersey
Francis Hopkinson	38, Lawyer, New Jersey
Richard Stockton	45, Lawyer, New Jersey
John Witherspoon	53, Clergyman, New Jersey
William Floyd	41, Landowner, New York
Francis Lewis	63, Merchant, New York
Philip Livingston	60, Merchant, New York
Lewis Morris	50, Landowner, New York
Joseph Hewes	46, Merchant, North Carolina
William Hooper	34, Lawyer, North Carolina
John Penn	36, Lawyer, North Carolina
George Clymer	37, Merchant, Pennsylvania
Benjamin Franklin	70, Printer/Statesman, Pennsylvania
Robert Morris	42, Merchant, Pennsylvania
John Morton	51, Surveyor/Judge, Pennsylvania
George Ross	46, Lawyer, Pennsylvania
Benjamin Rush	30, Physician, Pennsylvania
James Smith	56, Lawyer, Pennsylvania
George Taylor	60, Ironmaster[31], Pennsylvania
James Wilson	33, Lawyer, Pennsylvania
William Ellery	48, Lawyer, Rhode Island
Stephen Hopkins	69, Merchant/Politician, Rhode Island
Thomas Heyward, Jr.	30, Lawyer/Planter, South Carolina
Thomas Lynch, Jr.	27, Planter, South Carolina
Arthur Middleton	34, Planter, South Carolina

[31] Ironmaster: Owner or manager of an ironworks

Edward Rutledge	26, Lawyer, South Carolina
Carter Braxton	36, Planter, Virginia
Benjamin Harrison	50, Planter, Virginia
Thomas Jefferson	33, Lawyer/Planter, Virginia
Frances Lightfoot Lee	41, Planter, Virginia
Richard Henry Lee	44, Politician/Planter, Virginia
Thomas Nelson, Jr.	37, Planter, Virginia
George Wythe	50, Lawyer, Virginia

Figure 30:
The Memorial to the 56 Signers of the Declaration of Independence is on Signers Island in Constitution Gardens, Washington, D.C.

Index

Thank you for buying this guide to the Declaration of Independence. If you enjoyed reading it and found it informative, please consider leaving a review.

Happy Semiquincentennial 2026!

Printed by Amazon Italia Logistica S.r.l.
Torrazza Piemonte (TO), Italy

74869988R00038